Life in a Medieval Town

Life in a
Medieval Town

PETER HAMMOND

AMBERLEY PUBLISHING

First published in the United Kingdom in 2008 by
Amberley Publishing
Cirencester Road · Chalford · Stroud · Gloucestershire · GL6 8PE
www.amberley-books.com

British Library Cataloguing in Publication Data.
A catalogue record for this book is available from the British Library.

ISBN 978 1 84868 126 2

Typesetting and origination by
Amberley Publishing Plc.
Printed and bound in England.

Contents

Introduction

The term 'middle ages' is a rather vague one and for the purposes of this book I have taken it to be the late middle ages, from about the beginning of the thirteenth to the end of the fifteenth century. Town life changed all the time of course but these three centuries can be taken as reasonably homogenous. The incidents and way of life described in the following pages do not describe life in any particular town but are a composite picture. I hope and believe that it presents a picture of life which would be recognised by any townsman or woman from that period.

As usual with my books I am as indebted as ever to Carolyn, my wife, who is my sternest critic and want to thank her both for reading the manuscript and for encouraging my writing of it. I believe that this book is better for her comments although any faults remain mine.

CHAPTER 1

The Town Day

Public life in towns began very early, at dawn in fact, with the ringing of the Angelus bell at five or six o'clock. This was the signal for the first mass of the day. Sometimes the start of the working day was signalled by a special watch bell, but in most towns it was the mass bell. At this signal early travellers who wished to hear a mass before setting off on the dangerous business of travel would be coming into the streets to attend mass or at least say a prayer and the townspeople knew it was time to rise and start work.

At about the same time the town gates were opened to allow in traders and early rising country dwellers. Non-citizens would usually have to pay a toll. Cattle were driven in (mostly for milk as well as some for meat) and even geese in the later middle ages. The number of cattle needed for food in even a moderate size town was very large, for a town with a population of about 8,000 for example perhaps as many as 6,000 sheep and 30,000 pigs per year would be needed. Large amounts of grain in carts would be driven through the streets or delivered by river if there was one available.

The townsfolk were also astir early. The pigs kept penned up at night were released, some of them to be driven outside the walls to their grazing grounds but many if not most would be allowed to forage in the streets, of which more later. Tradesmen would be opening their shops or workshops. Blacksmiths in particular often opened at dawn because early travellers might require their services and butchers were likewise early risers because they would want to have an opportunity to butcher their cattle and prepare it for sale before too many customers were about. Sometimes butchers tried to begin work before daylight which had to be forbidden by regulation. Slaughtering beasts would inevitably have caused considerable noise so it would be understandable for a very early start to be unpopular. The same might well have applied to blacksmiths but perhaps they did not generally try to begin at unearthly hours. The London wiresellers apparently sometimes also tried to begin before the hour of five, the time at which they were allowed to begin in the winter but had to be stopped because their 'knocking, filing or any other noiseful work whereby [their] neighbours and others of the kings people might be annoyed or discomforted'. In the summer when everyone got up earlier they were allowed to begin when they wished.

The majority of shops and small businesses began work at about six. These were almost all small businesses with staff very often living in. Breakfast was taken as soon after rising as possible or after the first mass of the day for those who attended. They would thus be on the premises and opening early would be no problem. Markets usually opened at 'prime', a vague term which probably meant at six like the shops. Town residents were allowed to buy the goods at this time before retailers and street traders were allowed to buy large quantities for resale.

It would have been after about nine o'clock when the markets and shops had all opened that the noise and the bustle and crowding of the town streets would have reached a maximum. There were people pushing here and there, carts trying to get through the crowds and adding to the noise with the horses' hooves and the iron shod wheels ringing on the cobbles or paving of the better streets. The crowds made more noise than we are used to, workmen were singing at their jobs and itinerant salesmen and women were calling out their wares. There was considerable noise coming from the shops (with apprentices calling out their wares) and from the many small workshops where noise arising from the process going on within would be clearly audible in the street. In general the street noise apparently roused little complaint although sometimes complaints were made that worshippers in churches were being disturbed. In one case in London, fruit and vegetable sellers became accustomed to standing outside the church of St Austin. The priests complained they could not hear themselves singing mass and that the crowd of traders prevented the congregation from getting into or out of the church. The traders were forced to move elsewhere.

The noise from the many church bells was always present, calling the attention of worshippers to the many church services, the passing bell would ring to signify that someone was about to die, bells signalled a funeral, others the start of a mass or the sacring bell at the elevation of the host. They probably all attracted little attention except when they were taken as a time signal (see below under Religion). Sometimes a bell was rung to summon freemen to a meeting of the Common Council. This might be a bell on the guild hall itself or a particular church bell which was always used for this. Sometimes a bell would ring as an alarm, it might be to warn of a fire.

By noon the streets became quieter. A meal was sometimes taken about now, or even earlier, starting work at dawn must have meant that everyone became hungry well before noon. Building workers, who were to some extent different in their organisation to most other trades, usually stopped for a meal and a sleep at noon but then they always worked from dawn to dusk. Other less hard working trades stopped work earlier and would eat their afternoon meal about four o'clock or later, nearer dusk and vespers. In the afternoon as the light began to fail many shops would close although this did not apply universally since cookshops, tavern keepers and itinerant food sellers would often continue until about nine o'clock. Barbers and blacksmiths similarly would stay open until late, hoping for custom from late travellers. They were warned when it was time to stop by the ringing of the curfew bell at about nine o'clock. After this the town gates were closed and no one was allowed in or out. Townsfolk now felt secure and safe in their beds. After the curfew was rung no one apart from the night watchmen was allowed to be out in the streets unless carrying a lantern and of good repute. The town then rested until the whole noisy cycle started again the next morning.

CHAPTER 2

Town Government

How was this noisy crowded town governed? Towns were built on trade and the way they were run was designed to enable them to trade more efficiently, the elite citizens were the richer merchants and the merchants governed the town. The merchants were supported or sometimes opposed by the craft guilds into which the craftsmen were mostly organised. The citizens of the town governed under a charter, usually from the king, giving them the power to regulate their own affairs without the interference of any superior lord. The charter allowed the citizens to elect a mayor, and to form a council through which they acted. The town authorities regulated the prices and the quality of goods, saw that weights and measures were as the law prescribed and checked business practices. The town electors were those who were freemen of the town, usually this meant full members of their craft guild. Freedom could be inherited, if your father was a freeman then you had a right to freedom too, a rule which always applied to men and occasionally to women as well. Apprentices who had served out their apprenticeship and worked for some time as journeymen were allowed to become freemen on the payment of a small fee, or freedom could be purchased by immigrants to the town for a larger fee. Freedom was desirable because a freeman was allowed to trade in the town without paying tolls. Other town dwellers could buy the right to trade as an annual licence. Freemen had the right to participate in the political life of the town. All freemen of the town participated in the guild and city elections but frequently the mayor and aldermen who actually ran the town were really elected (or selected) by a small self perpetuating group, that of the wealthier members of the merchant community. Once a freeman had become a member of the ruling group, be it by being a member of the right family or by becoming a man who was wealthy and influential enough to be of use to the town and its rulers, he could rise steadily through the offices available. In large towns, those that had received a royal grant making them a county in their own right, the town held its own court presided over by the sheriff, their monetary affairs were controlled by the chamberlain, and the aldermen acted as town council and elected the mayor who ruled overall. The court was a criminal court as well as policing the numerous regulations handed down from the king's court, such as enforcing the market regulations. Lesser men were needed to act as clerks to the courts or as ale tasters, constables, bridge wardens, gatekeepers, gaolers and so on. A large town needed a large number of workers to keep their bureaucracy going so that the business of merchants making money could go on smoothly.

The trade guilds were important in the government of the town and in maintaining the standards of the craft. Guilds were regulated by the council because of their influence and because the guild searchers were responsible for enforcing trade regulations and standards (see below). This gave them great influence. Guilds were important too for keeping good relations between their members and workers, trade suffered if workers were restless. The guilds also vouched for the standards of their members if necessary and regulated the hours worked. They provided mutual support for them too. Members of a guild would meet at least once a year to elect officers and to audit accounts and new members would be inducted at these times and new ordinances discussed. Another important activity was the guild feasts which were held regularly.

Women were rarely members of guilds. This was on the basis that they were not formally trained and could not become a master of the trade. Since most men would not take on and train a woman this meant that they could never become eligible. Women were sometimes trained informally by their fathers or husbands though and their work was always important. They were sometimes allowed to carry on the trade of their husband if they were widowed and some trades such as the brewers often had women brewsters. Women were in fact frequently involved in the food trades, making or selling the products. In general women were paid much less than a man doing a similar job. Women frequently helped their husbands in some way to run a workshop or shop and were recognised as a key part of the workforce. Even so, most of the work carried out by women tended to lie in skills which were an extension of household tasks such as cooking (as noted above) or needlework and knitting.

CHAPTER 3

The Streets

The medieval town was a cramped and crowded place mostly still within its walls, of which the citizens were very proud. Most of the streets were very narrow and were unpaved. The very poorest streets were just paved with beaten earth or earth and vegetable matter such as straw. Better streets had a layer of sand and gravel and more important streets had sand and cobbles. The streets were divided into a footpath on each side of a central gutter which was supposed to take away rain water. Each householder was responsible for maintaining the path outside his house up to the gutter in the middle and sometimes the goods of the householder would be seized if he or she did not carry out the repairs. It was very difficult to get townsmen to repair the street, or at least to get them to make adequate repairs so that towns increasingly made themselves responsible. When they did so a toll known as pavage was levied on 'foreigners', i.e. non citizens coming into town with goods to sell. The amount paid was ruled by the weight of the goods and the type of vehicle the merchant was using. This meant that those with iron shod wheels to their wagons which caused more wear and tear paid more than wooden wheeled wagons. Pedestrians usually paid nothing particularly if they were only carrying personal goods. The tax thus raised went to street repairs. Further money was raised by bequests in wills to maintain a particular street or streets. The men employed to repair streets were known as paviours and a trained man received good wages.

Since it would not usually have been possible to close a road completely, the paving method used by houeholders or the paviours was probably usually to do little more than to loosen the surface on one side and then the other (or just in front of the owner's house), remove a small part and then lay down sand or gravel or whatever the new surface was and perhaps lay stone on top. They would then ram the surface firm with a heavy hand rammer. This would not have made the new surface very long lasting and on a street with heavy traffic the surface must have broken up again fairly quickly. Iron wheeled carts damaged the surfaces more quickly than wooden wheeled ones but both caused problems. Sledges were almost always frowned upon. The poor tamping down of the new surface would also mean that there was a risk of the new surface ending up higher than the surrounding older surface with the result that the whole street slowly rose. Householders carrying out their own repairs were enjoined very firmly not to allow this to happen. Professional pavers would also take care to slope the path down to the central gutter to provide drainage but householders did not take so much care with the result that the surface water drained into the houses.

As well as repairing the streets householders were originally responsible for cleaning that part of it outside their own house, down to the gutter. Whether or not they had done this was checked by an official scavenger appointed for the purpose and attempts were made to ensure that everyone cleaned their part of the street at least once a week. Of course it was only too easy for householders to move rubbish from outside their house to outside their neighbour's house. This practice was greatly frowned upon. Heavy rain would sometimes do this for a householder, sweeping the rubbish away and leaving it further down the street. It must always have been unpleasant to walk in the streets but apart from special occasions the city authorities seem to have made no great effort to keep the streets clean. Only on such occasions as the knowledge that the funeral procession of Henry V would be going through the streets of London in 1422 with many dignitaries following on foot did the authorities make an effort to actually clean the streets. Sometimes a town would appoint an official street sweeper to carry out the cleaning. It was important to keep the central gutter clear and either the cleaner or an official known as a raker would do this. These officials were not above diverting the water in the gutter so that in a storm rubbish they had not cleared would be swept to another street which was the responsibility of another raker.

The parts of the town which could not be allocated to a householder for cleaning, such as the market square, the parts between houses or opposite empty buildings were always cleaned by the town authorities as were the spaces around the town gates. Towns sometimes also paved and cleaned the area around the guildhall. As time went on the towns gradually assumed responsibility for repairing the streets. This meant that in general streets became better kept, since enforcing the previous system was very difficult and always meant that streets were generally not repaired or were very patchy at best.

Narrow streets caused more than problems with repairs and basic cleaning. Householders left rubbish in the streets or even stored their property there. In the latter case it would usually be something heavy so that it could not easily be stolen. Building materials were often piled outside the houses, householders were sometimes only allowed three days to do this before they had to be moved. Builders were allowed more leeway. Shopkeepers sometimes tried (illegally) to extend their trading space by putting tables outside their shop and to place market stalls outside the proper market area. Other encroachments on the street were more substantial. House owners often tried building penthouses sticking out over the street onto their buildings. This was usually allowed provided it was not so low that a cart could not pass underneath. Building an extension lower than this seems rather unreasonable. New buildings at ground level were not allowed to go over the building line although house owners tried to get away with this too. Dangerous or ruinous buildings could be destroyed and the owner fined, particularly if he had ignored warnings to put it into a better state of repair. Dangerous trees, whether on someone's property or not could be chopped down if they looked liable to fall and cause damage to property or passers by. The wood was sold for the benefit of the town.

The chaos, the noise and indeed the smell in the narrow, untidy and badly repaired streets of these small towns must have been immediately obvious. Much of life, human and animal, was lived in the streets, the open fronted shops would look part of the street, there were crowds of people going about their business or just standing about and talking, many street sellers were calling out their wares and then there were the animals including chickens and omnipresent pigs (see below). This must have made the street seem rather like a farmyard. Temporary obstructions were common, not just the piles of refuse, but sometimes tradesmen's stalls in the street and not in the proper market place, or tables placed outside a shop. Both of these were strictly forbidden because they were often an attempt to avoid paying stallage, the market toll, or were put up by traders from outside the town who were supposed to carry their goods about with them unless they paid for a licence to have a market stall.

Congestion in the main streets cannot have been helped by carts or porters carrying goods to and from market although having to stop and pay a toll at the town gate would help prevent build up in the streets at least in the early morning. Sometimes 'foreigners' (non residents) had to trade at a different time to citizens and this would help relieve overcrowding too. Driving horses through the streets to water, that is not leading them on a rein, was forbidden because of the danger to passers-by, particularly children playing in the streets. It was forbidden in London to drive carts faster when unloaded because of the danger to others. Unattended horses could be seized by any passing constable and the owner made to pay a fine. There were very many horses in towns of course because as well as being used to pull carts they were also used for transport by those who could afford to keep them or hire them for a journey. Few could buy a horse both because of the initial capital cost and the cost of feeding and stabling. Also, the average citizen would not need one for journeys in a town which might only be twenty minutes walk from one side to the other. Pack horses or horses pulling the many carts needed to bring goods into the town were a frequent sight, carts seeming usually to have been pulled by two horses or even three. This was partly because medieval horses were noticeably smaller and less powerful than modern horses and would look to our eyes more like sturdy ponies.

Pigs were undoubtedly the greatest animal nuisance in the streets. They were kept by most townsfolk as a useful source of meat, and since many householders had minimal or no garden space they were frequently allowed to roam in the street to root in the gutter and eat what they could find. This saved the cost of feeding them and each owner must have had some way of marking his or her pig so as to be able to distinguish it from that of their neighbour. The pigs seem to have caused so much trouble with rooting through rubbish heaps and diving under stalls to pick up tasty morsels and doubtless causing nasty accidents that most towns forbade owners from allowing their pigs to roam in the street. Owners were sometimes warned that anyone who kept a pig must keep it at home and any pig found roaming in the town could be caught and killed. In this case the owner had the right to buy the dead pig. In Bristol the tail was cut off on a first offence, thus identifying a transgressing pig, only cutting off the head at a second offence. The fact that there were so many ordinances against pigs probably meant that in no town was enforcing the rule taken very seriously and that usually pigs wandered about as they pleased.

There was no real attempt to control dogs in the same way. In general they were expected to be kept on a chain if out on the street with their owner, but guard dogs were tolerated unless they were vicious and in any case were expected to be locked up at night. There must however have been many masterless dogs wandering the streets.

An ever present contribution to the frequent noisomeness of the streets was provided by smoke. In general in the middle ages, coal (or sea coal as it was known) was not used by householders since brick chimneys were not common and coal burns at too high a temperature to be used with a wooden chimney. It was however used by lime burners and in brick kilns. Lime and brick kilns produce unpleasant fumes and owners who attempted to build them in the town, as occasionally happened, were usually ordered not to build them anywhere near on the pain of a large fine. Smoke in general was regarded as a problem and householders were fined if their smoke was regularly causing problems for others.

Adding to the problems in the streets was the fact that there was no drainage apart from surface drains and that most people had nowhere to throw rubbish except into the street. Town regulations frequently fulminated against dung heaps in the streets, although there must indeed have been a great deal of dung dropped from the many animals passing through. To add to the mess, many people threw water (and worse) from their windows into the street. Fishmongers too sometimes threw water out after they had washed their fish: this would be the fishmongers who had not washed them in the

public water supply, as some were known to do.
Towns tried to prevent this too, but must have largely
failed. Water in the streets from the vats of the dyers
was particularly disliked. This is not surprising since
as well as using a great deal of water they also used
stale urine as part of their dyeing process.

Town and city authorities also made efforts to
control the environmental problems posed by the
large numbers of traders selling perishable goods such
as meat. Butchers were particularly heavily regulated
since they produced a great deal of very nasty
rubbish in many forms including offal. Sometimes
as well as bringing their cattle into the town through
the streets producing droppings, they slaughtered
them in the street and left the non usable pieces
there afterwards, the usable by-products such as hides
and horns being sold on their own account. In some
towns the butchers were ordered to throw their waste
into a particular part of the local river, downstream
from any point of use of the water. The butchers
in the London Shambles, made a great nuisance of

1. How a medieval city might have looked from a distance with the walls and the church towers the most prominent features. South west prospect of the city of York, by John Haynes, *c*.1731. *Published by permission of the York Museums Trust (York Art Gallery)*

2. A medieval gate with barbican in front which protected the gate itself. This gate is Mickelgate Bar, York. The Barbican was demolished in 1829

3. A medieval town scene with a shop front (the artist must mean the shop to be a bakery) and an inn sign above. *Reproduced by permission from* The Arrival, *a painting by Graham Turner (www.studio88.co.uk)*

4. The Shambles in York, a street which still looks much as it must have done in the middle ages when it was a centre of the butchery trade with overhanging houses almost touching in places

5. Merchants unloading goods from ships. A modern window in the Merchant Adventurer's Hall, York. *Photographed by kind permission of the Company of Merchant Adventurers of the City of York*

6. Merchant stall selling fish, dating from about 1417. The customer is wearing pattens to keep his shoes out of mud. A redrawing of a street scene from Constance, Germany. *(Concilium Constantiense, St Petersburg, 1874)*

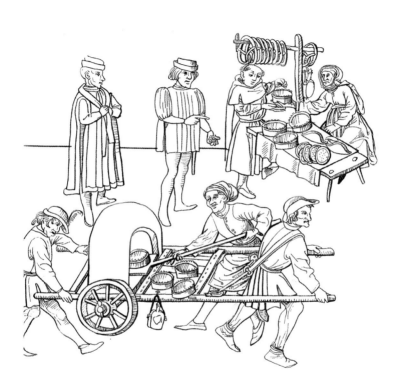

7. Market stall selling bread and pies and what seems to be a stall with a portable oven selling pies, perhaps one of the licensed street sellers, about 1417. A redrawing of a street scene from Constance, Germany. *(Concilium Constantiense, St Petersburg, 1874)*

8. The great hall in a town house showing communal eating arrangements, with the high table for the lord on the left. Barley Hall, York.

themselves in the fourteenth century by using a quay on the river Fleet to clean the entrails of the beasts they had slaughtered. They also frequently threw the entrails onto the pavement outside the house of the Grey Friars. Attempts were made to force them to clean the entrails elsewhere, without success. This lack of success in making butchers obey the law was a common problem and eventually butchers were forbidden to slaughter beasts in towns.

In fact, concerning the disposal of entrails it could almost be said that most of the town inhabitants disposed of them in inappropriate places. Housewives certainly did so and professional cooks also sometimes threw the entrails of poultry into the street. Poulterers caused an indescribable mess and smell at the places where they kept their birds, 'whereof the ordure and standing of them is of great stench and so evil savour that it causeth great and parlous infecting of the people' as the London regulations put it. To compound their sins when the Poulterers plucked their birds they made no attempt to stop the feathers escaping and blowing about. The fishmongers seem in general to have been more law abiding, or less messy at least, and did not cause so much of this kind of nuisance, apart from (as noted earlier) sometimes washing their fish in the common water conduit. They certainly sold a very large variety and quantity of fish both sea and freshwater as well as salted fish. Much fish was required because it was eaten on fast days and in the Lenten period.

Although people sometimes dumped whole dead animals in the streets (when not throwing them over the town walls or into the river) which must have made the streets rather hazardous to walk through, the major problem of street dumping was probably (as noticed earlier) the large amount of animal dung that was deposited. It was not just pigs: dogs, goats and horses all contributed their share. There will have been a lot of dung outside houses because of the need to get rid of dung from the chickens kept by most householders, from the pigs which were kept by most (or allowed to wander in the street) and from the horses, which some would keep. Towns often tried to control the amount accumulating outside houses. Some allowed it to accumulate for a week before it had to be removed, while others forbade any dung at all to be thrown into the street on pain of a substantial fine. It is difficult to believe that this meant that no dung was left to pile up. In some towns, households had to organise a cart to take away their rubbish and dung, or the town arranged for a cart and collected payment for the service. Of course however the dung and the rubbish were removed from the houses and from the town it had ultimately to be disposed of somewhere. Originally it would all have been disposed of in the town ditch or in the local river but as towns increased in size it became more important to provide for sites away from the walls to avoid noisome smells in the city. It was nearly always forbidden for anyone to tip nasty rubbish in the river except at particular places down river from the town.

A problem which could not be solved by moving

tipping places away from the town was the disposal of human waste. As populations grew this became an increasing problem. There was no drainage from houses and many had cesspits in the garden or a cellar from which all such waste had to be physically removed in some way. There were 'gong farmers' (a gong was a privy) who would empty such pits although they made an understandably high charge to do so and were not allowed to carry the ordure through the streets before nine o'clock in the evening. Houses built over or near to a river often did not have a cesspit but used a private channel to the river. This meant that the river became increasingly polluted. In the case of smaller rivers this rapidly became unacceptable and the river was eventually bricked or paved over as happened in the case of the Walbrook in London. This did not necessarily stop people living near it using the river underneath but it would have made it more difficult. Public latrines did exist in towns, and sometimes these were provided by public spirited citizens. They sometimes became a nuisance and were ordered to be moved outside the walls. This cannot really have improved matters and would in any case remove them from within the walls where they were actually needed. These public facilities were sometimes quite large, one in London, built at the expense of Dick Whittington as one of his many charitable works, was known as 'Whittington's longhouse' and consisted of two rows of sixty-four seats, one for men and one for women. It was built over the Thames and was flushed by the tide. Above were five rooms for pensioners of the parish, perhaps not the best place to live.

The health of citizens was undoubtedly affected by the unhygienic conditions in towns, epidemic diseases struck regularly and infant mortality was high throughout the period. However as more councils began to take control of cleaning and provided more clean water, cleanliness certainly improved and probably health did too towards the end of the middle ages. Before this those who fell sick as a result of the laissez faire attitude towards hygiene were cared for in several ways. In the home the housewife was responsible. She was expected to know the basic first aid techniques, be able to bandage simple wounds and to know the herbs which cured simple ailments. If she could afford it for more serious illnesses she could consult an apothecary or a woman healer. She could also take the patient to a barber surgeon who would let blood, a cure for most things in the medieval mind. There were doctors who could deal adequately with wounds and injuries, unless the wound became infected, but who could do little for serious illness and in any case their fees would be too high for most households. Nothing could be done in the case of severe illness such as typhoid and the chance of an epidemic raging through the town was an ever present risk. There were hospitals, run by religious orders, staffed by monks or nuns and lay nurses, who had a good basic knowledge of medicine and took in anyone. They gave the patients good care and peace, and as important, the assurance that they were seeking the intervention of God in their case, which the sick knew was an essential part of healing.

CHAPTER 4

Houses

The houses in the narrow streets were packed very closely together and the houses were themselves fairly narrow with a frontage of perhaps fifteen to eighteen feet often with a long piece of land to the rear. This arrangement meant that as many houses as possible could be fitted along a busy street. Sometimes if there was pressure on space for new houses speculators subdivided plots into even narrower ones. If a town was shrinking in size, as happened after the Black Death, then the opposite took place and plots were merged to make them bigger and there were empty plots or houses. A few houses of the wealthy were built of stone (and the town records sometimes noted the fact of a house being 'the stone house') but most houses were built of strong wood frames and laths with plaster filling in the gaps between the wood frames. Brick was not common until after the end of the middle ages. The tallest buildings to be seen were the town guildhall if it had one and the many churches rising above their surroundings. In the poorer parts of the town where widows and single people lived there were often only small single storey buildings. However not all houses in the wealthier parts of a town were large or lived in by the wealthy. Smaller houses were often wedged between larger houses, with richer townsfolk living next to poorer ones. Most houses and shops were rented – only the rich could own their own house.

The single storey houses of the poor were very small and cramped and probably dirty and smelly too. Sometimes they consisted of a single room only but more often had at least two, the front being used as a shop. These poorer houses were wattle and daub (a mixture of clay, dung and straw) between wooden frames. They were often thatched with rye or wheat straw although thatch was frowned upon by town authorities because of the danger of fire (see below).

The houses of better off people were larger, on a long narrow plot with one gable end fronting on to the street and the rest of the house stretching back down the plot with one room behind the other. There was a yard at the back sometimes separating a kitchen from the rest of the house, this was to try to stop fire from spreading, the kitchen might well contain the largest or the only large open fire in the house and so would be the place most likely to be a source of conflagration. Behind the kitchen, if there was space, was a narrow garden. The front room in any house was mostly used for a shop or a workshop with a storehouse or office behind. Above these rooms were one or two more storeys which were used for eating and sleeping. The upper floors often jutted out over the street. This gave more floor space on these floors but unfortunately made it easier for fire to spread since at this level the opposite sides of the street sometimes almost touched.

The houses of wealthy people were larger still. They had a wider front than the houses of lesser folk and were sometimes as much as thirty or forty feet wide. These larger houses might have a courtyard and a large hall on the ground floor. Small tradesmen did not need a hall such as this but households with more pretensions needed one to dine in, to entertain important guests and to accommodate the increasing numbers of staff a wealthier person needed to show their status. The hall went up two storeys, sometimes to a fine roof. In early times a hall had a central fire with a louvre in the roof to let out the smoke. When wall fireplaces and chimneys became popular later, the smoke in a hall with the old fashioned system must have sometimes made eating or just living in the hall very difficult. Behind the hall was a screens passage, separating the hall from the kitchen and pantry and above these were perhaps a solar, a private chamber for the family to retire to and sometimes their bedchamber too. In the houses of wealthier citizens there might be another wing to the house containing a grand bedchamber for the master of the household with lesser rooms underneath for storage. These rooms gave a little privacy to the master and mistress and their family but there was little privacy in general for lesser members of a household.

Later the hall was sometimes placed on the first floor with a shop and store houses underneath. The use of a chimney was extended to the kitchen and the chimney could be used to service a fireplace in the solar and hall above. In the solar or just off it there was often a privy, with a wooden chute connecting it to the cesspit outside (or sometimes inside) the house. Lesser households used chamber pots. The cesspit was usually made of stone but occasionally older ones of wood remained in use. These cesspits were large and ten feet or more deep. Since the houses were close together there were frequently disputes between neighbours about cesspits leaking into a neighbour's house, sometimes into their cellar if they had one. The cesspits were emptied infrequently and must have been very noisome.

As well as a privy, solars frequently had a window, an unusual luxury. Lesser houses just had window openings with shutters to fill them at night or when it was cold. The window space might contain a fenestral, that is a lattice frame containing fabric coated with resin and tallow which let in light, kept out drafts and was removable in fine weather. Only very wealthy people had glass in their windows. These were frequently in removable frames so that they could be transported to other houses of the owner and to prevent theft while a house was empty.

None of these houses contained a great deal of furniture. All except the very poorest had a table, usually a trestle table which could if necessary be taken down and stored against a wall to create more space. There would be benches and stools to sit on, with probably at least one chair for the master of the house to use. Nearly all houses, particularly those with some pretensions, would have at least one chest and possibly more than one in which to store linen and clothing and papers as well as a stronger coffer in which to keep valuables – if any. There might be small cupboards to store food and shelves for cups, bowls, jugs, and trenchers – flat pieces of wood or metal, used as plates. The richer the household the more furniture it had, but no household had a great deal. Richer men would have a buffet in the hall on which to display any plate they had in order to impress visitors and buying plate was a way of storing wealth too. All households had some kitchen equipment, which might include cooking pots, a frying pan, cooking spoons and a spit and had table implements, knives to eat with (although most men carried their own eating knife) and spoons. Forks were not used in the middle ages. In the rooms in which the poor people slept the only beds were pallets which were bags filled with straw, dried fern or heather. This was all servants in any house could hope for. Wealthier people had wooden bedsteads in their bedrooms on which was placed a mattress probably similar to a pallet. Very wealthy people had a canopied or hung bed, probably with a feather filled mattress and surrounded by curtains, much more comfortable. All furniture was painted to decorate it, sometimes very elaborately.

In these streets of largely wooden houses fire was greatly feared and precautions were taken to avoid or mitigate an outbreak. Carelessness was very often the cause, straw mattresses near a fire caught alight only too easily and a drunkard sleeping on a straw mattress with a lighted candle next to him was an equal hazard. It seems that keeping straw near to fires, perhaps due to little spare space, was a prolific source of fires. Since the main problem was that most houses were inflammable, there was not a lot that could be done to prevent fire, but towns did what they could. Thatched roofs were banned in many towns and householders were only allowed to use shingles or wooden boards as a minimum requirement with tiles or stone if they could afford them. Roofs were supposed to be plastered on the inside to help prevent fire getting through. In London it was forbidden to have chimneys made from wood; instead they were supposed to be made from stone or plaster or other non flammable substances.

Cooking was a prolific source of unforeseen fires

since all cooks, from the housewife to cook shops, had to use open fires to cook on or to heat ovens. Householders were expected to have safe ovens and sometimes were forbidden to use anything other than charcoal or wood as fuel. That is they were not allowed to use straw, fern or reeds as fuel since these could flare up suddenly and generate great heat or float up a chimney while alight. This particularly applied to professional cooks. Poorer people often had no oven and would take their bread to be baked by local bakers thus avoiding at least that fire hazard. In London from a very early date to minimise risks cook shops were expected to be plastered inside and out and whitewashed as well as not having internal partitions. This regulation was made after a disastrous fire and had nothing to do with hygiene although it may have helped with this. This applied as well to brewers and bakers who were also users of large fires. As well as the building regulations other fire precautions were taken, particularly in the summer or in times of drought when a vessel of water was expected to be stationed outside the doors of all houses. The guildhall and larger houses kept fire hooks, that is strong crooks of iron with wooden handles, stored in the eaves of the houses which had them and which would be used to pull off the burning roof of a building. Chains and strong ropes were used to pull down houses around an outbreak to try and contain the fire. When a fire broke out at night the watch would blow a horn and the bells of neighbouring churches were rung. The watch then organised helpers with leather buckets into a chain between the fire and the nearest source of water. This might be a well, conduit or sometimes the wagon of a water carrier. Buckets and ladders were brought by householders who owned them. Not a lot could be done to put out a large fire since there were no pumps and there is a limit to the amount of water that can be thrown from a bucket. Usually fires would burn themselves out sometimes having caused a great deal of damage. The most that householders could hope for was to rescue anyone trapped by the fire and to save valuables.

CHAPTER 5

Law and Order

There was no regular police force in the medieval town and the keeping of the peace in the streets was largely the responsibility of the inhabitants. They were aided and encouraged by various groups of officials, sergeants, petty constables and beadles. These had wide powers but since they were few in number needed the help of the citizens to make a difference. The sergeants were most akin to the modern police and acted as an armed group when needed. With most men going armed, if only with a long dagger, a disturbance could easily turn into a riot when force would be needed to restore the peace. Usually one or two of their number acted as sergeants at mace in civic processions, walking before the mayor carrying the town maces, the symbols of authority. Sergeants were sometimes used as gatekeepers of the town. Not all towns, particularly smaller ones, had beadles. Where they existed beadles sometimes had their authority restricted, as in London, to operating within a particular ward and reporting contraventions of regulations to the alderman of that ward although they would deal with minor infringements of the law themselves or with the help of the constables. The constables were men of lesser authority and were subordinate to beadles and sergeants but were greater in number – they were the foot soldiers of the policing force. They were probably always men of good physique.

Since they were relatively few in number the effectiveness of these forces depended on the cooperation of the citizens of the town. When someone raised a hue and cry all able bodied men and women were expected to join in the chase after a suspected criminal. Anyone seeing something suspicious happening could raise the hue and cry and chase the culprit. If they were the first to catch the suspect they could arrest him or her and if necessary take the culprit to prison, although normally a constable would do this. Any citizen who refused to take part in the hue or even withdrew without permission could be fined. The duty of chasing a suspect was sometimes followed by another duty, that of watching that the suspect did not escape from sanctuary. If a suspect could reach a church or other place recognised as a sanctuary, that is somewhere a criminal could stop and rest without fear of arrest, he was allowed to stay there for forty days and nights. Most parish churches and greater religious houses were allowed to function as sanctuaries. As a suspected criminal the sanctuary man was watched to make sure that he did not leave. If he was caught sneaking out he could be arrested, if he stayed until the end of the forty days he had to abjure the realm, that is go into exile, first confessing his crime. He was not allowed ever to return on pain of execution. The duty to watch a sanctuary was a very unpopular one, it had to be kept up night and day and must have been very difficult to organise.

Citizens were also expected to serve on the watch at night. They were sometimes chosen according to a rota and sometimes it seems to have been more random. However the men were chosen there were fines for not attending. If a chosen citizen refused to attend the sergeant organising the watch was allowed to hire a substitute and charge the recalcitrant citizen next morning. Substitutes were allowed but had to be able bodied and armed. Sending someone who could not actually do the job was not allowed. Exemptions were sometimes allowed and it is very unlikely that substantial citizens were expected to serve.

The watch was frequently divided into groups, one group to watch at various points in the town and another or others to circulate through the town. Since they were not professional soldiers or police the watch seems frequently to have progressed around the town in a noisy and undisciplined manner. This would effectively conceal their own nervousness and also have the effect of making certain that would be criminals concealed themselves before the watch appeared.

Apart from the watch men were not allowed to bear arms at all at night, indeed night walking, particularly without carrying a light, was generally forbidden after the curfew bell at about ten o'clock at night. Naturally anyone with a good reason, doctors attending a sick patient or a priest hurrying to a dying person were allowed out and those of higher social standing were not questioned but anyone else without very good reason for being out at night was liable to be arrested and put into prison to await questioning in the morning. The night watch certainly was not redundant, records of thieves taken after curfew are common. Their activities when described by the record are such as might be expected, burglars climbing over walls or breaking through house walls or men who climbed up to roof level and removed lead pipes and guttering.

The bearing of arms was strictly regulated at all times. Violence was never very far beneath the surface in the middle ages and arguments frequently escalated and could involve crossbows, bows, swords, knives and cudgels. In fact most weapons known upon medieval battlefields were used at some point in the streets of a town somewhere in England. Sergeants and watchmen were protected by law from violence upon their person when engaged in making an arrest and citizens were expected to help them but the legal situation cannot have protected anyone in the midst of a violent riot in the streets.

Another aspect of law and order which exercised the mediaeval mind was the matter of public morality, that is prostitution. To some extent this was almost as much a matter of public order as public morality since brothels could be a source of unruly behaviour and crime and also a haven for criminals and criminal activity such as the receiving of stolen goods. Theoretically most towns did not allow prostitutes to live within the walls but this must have been very much ignored even in those towns such as London which allowed brothels to be opened across the river in Southwark, a semi-independent area at the south end of London Bridge, outside the jurisdiction of the city. The authorities may have hoped to make London a more salubrious place through this but it doesn't seem to have worked judging by the records of Cock Lane and other places in the city being well known as the haunts of prostitutes. The other common action of placing semi official brothels outside the walls of any town certainly never worked either. It is likely that prostitutes solicited in public places, the churchyard, the public houses and indeed the street. There were often regulations prohibiting such women from wearing rich clothing and, in some towns, forcing them to wear striped hoods. If it was necessary to do this it is obvious that they were often found in public. Additionally there are many records of women and men being presented before the courts for fornication. If a house was found to have been a brothel or even the house of a known prostitute, usually on information provided by neighbours, the doors and windows and sometimes the roof, could be removed. This would certainly make landlords careful to whom they rented property.

CHAPTER 6

Shops and Shopping

In the medieval town there was no shopping centre, shops were always interspersed with purely residential property although of course many shopkeepers lived on the premises anyway. There was always a concentration of food and drink sellers and taverns in the centre, which was both where the wealthy tended to live and where travellers and businessmen would chiefly need them. Such shops, together with tailors and shoemakers and other useful trades would also be scattered throughout the town. Shops were occasionally grouped as they are in a modern town because sometimes a builder erected a range of five or six one or two story buildings to be used as shops with a room behind the shop and a solar above in the bigger units.

The goods sold from these shops were of great variety and marketing, manufacturing and service industries could all be found, for example food suppliers of all kinds, including innkeepers, shoemakers, tailors, weavers and many kinds of smith. This was because towns in the middle ages had to be self sufficient, the townspeople expected to be able to get all their necessities and most of their luxuries there. Everything was made and sold at all stages of the process. Thus wool was woven into cloth by the weavers and dyed by the dyers. It was then made up into clothing by the tailors. The leatherworkers would prepare leather supplied by the tannery and make it up into gloves and belts and bags, and so on.

Shops serving one trade sometimes congregated together in the same part of the town. In many towns we still find a Butchers Row or a Shambles (originally slaughterhouses, by extension butchers shops), Fisher's Row, Milk street, Tanners Row and so on. Of course not only butchers had shops in Butchers Row and other tradesmen could and would have shops in the street, although this would not necessarily apply to the tanners. Tanning was (and is) a very smelly trade and probably most other traders would prefer not to be near a group of them even if they used their products. Sometimes trades grouped together because of similarities in their activities, for example armourers and sword smiths would often be close to the blacksmiths who would prepare the mild steel with from which they fashioned armour and weapons. The blacksmiths would themselves make the ploughshares, the nails, the wheel rims and the cooking pots needed for peaceful citizens. Thus towns of even modest size could provide all of the trades and products needed by everyone. Large towns had more specialised workers such as goldsmiths making gold and silver cups, jewels and rings, and other smiths such as bellmakers, kitchenware makers making small dishes and other smiths.

All of these goods were sold in shops which were open fronted establishments with a flap which folded down in front to form a counter. This was sometimes supported by two short posts. There was an awning or another flap above to protect the goods and perhaps also the customers. When the shop closed the front of the shop would be covered by the two flaps which were bolted from the inside to shut the interior of the shop off from the street. Most shops were very small, sometimes as small as five or six feet by ten feet, with grander ones having a frontage on the street of about twelve to eighteen feet, occasionally bigger. In the case of most shops there were living quarters and a workshop behind the shop, or in the case of the larger ones there were quarters above the shop. Sometimes the shop itself was also the workshop. These shops were cramped inside, although sometimes heavily stocked, and customers must frequently have only been able to stand outside in the street. Sometimes shops were simple lockups which were part of a larger house and rented out to the shopkeeper. Wealthy citizens often had several such shops in different parts of the town.

Most of these shops were run by the main industrial

unit in a town, the household. This was an extended household of a whole family plus their servants or staff. Most industry was thus on a very small scale with buying and selling all being done from the home premises of the owner of the business. Some men and women earned their living by working for others for daily wages, doing piece work, sometimes from their own home, sometimes by going out. Weaving could be done in this way for example, or women worked as seamstresses. Leather working where a number of different skills were needed and the work could be put out to piece workers lent itself to this system. Building work was almost all done by labourers working for daily wages.

Inside the shop was the master craftsman whose business it was, together with his apprentices and workers, who might include his wife and daughters. The total number varied according to the size of the business, sometimes only male relatives of the owner and his wife were involved in running the business. The master craftsman was almost always a member of his craft guild, as noted earlier and these guilds regulated his behaviour and the quality of his work, the hours worked and the working conditions. The lowest grade of members were the apprentices, bound to a master for a term of years to learn the trade while being fed and lodged by the master. After the apprentices in order of seniority came the journeymen who were freelance but qualified workers who had served an apprenticeship. They could become master craftsmen themselves if they were able to raise the capital required to set up business on their own, perhaps by marrying the daughter of their master. If they could not raise the capital they sometimes remained waged workers all their lives. Lastly in the hierarchy came the master who was recognised as such by the guild. The hours of work were long. The working day was always as long as the hours of daylight, or until the curfew bell which could be about the same time. A worker's day would thus be about sixteen hours in summer and about eleven in the winter. Meal breaks might come to about three hours in total for three meals. Breakfast was taken very early, not long after dawn, dinner was taken in the mid morning, probably not later than 10p.m. and supper perhaps at 4p.m. Sometimes breakfast was omitted and workmen occasionally had 'nuncheons', taken about the middle of the day.

When there were no customers the work, perhaps tailoring, was carried on in the front room behind the shop front all in full view of the passers by. When customers appeared one or more of the staff would come out into the street (the number going out perhaps depending on the apparent importance of the customer) and accost them more or less aggressively to persuade them to examine the goods or to come into the shop to see more of the goods. The staff were not supposed to be too overbearing to customers but obviously were on occasion because towns made regulations to prevent them from doing so. For example cooks were forbidden to grasp the sleeves of possible customers with their greasy and floury hands nor were shop workers supposed to talk to customers looking into the shop next door.

Not all goods were bought in shops, or the market (see below), there were many travelling salesmen, known as chapmen (or peddlers), who went through the streets from door to door selling small amounts of goods to housewives, or indeed anyone else who would buy. They bought goods in one place (frequently cloth) where it was cheapest and sold it elsewhere at a profit, buying in return small goods for sale to their customers. Some chapmen had an enormous stock with quite large quantities of many kinds of goods including such diverse things as gloves and caps, ribbons and mirrors as well as quantities of many kinds of spices. Most of their goods appealed to ordinary housewives and some of these might have bought small amounts of the spices for cooking but probably all chapmen had wealthier customers whom they visited and who would buy the more expensive goods, including spices.

CHAPTER 7

Food and Food shops

Food shops and shopping deserve a chapter to themselves because so many people, whatever their main occupations also sold food of some type, ale for example, to supplement their income. Also, everyone needed to buy food, it was something they all needed every day. Much of this food was bought from shops, as well as in the markets. Some food shops had a general stock, selling for example mustard, herrings, candles and other goods. Occasionally 'shops' were more like bazaars, where up to fifty traders all selling similar goods shared space in one large shed like area. In a very large town such as London shops selling meat, fish or bread would sell only their speciality but outside London, at least in the fifteenth century, bakers, butchers and fishmongers sold not only their own speciality but a wide range of other edible goods including cheese and butter.

Vegetables and fruit were often bought not from grocers' shops as nowadays, but sometimes from neighbours who grew them in their gardens and sold the surplus which was over and above what they needed. Sometimes owners of very large gardens sold direct to the market and there were always market gardens outside towns growing these goods commercially and bringing them to town to be sold in the market. All of the fruit and vegetables that we expect to buy were available, and some, such as primrose and groundsel, that we would not expect to be able to buy. Fruits such as apples, pears, cherries and nuts were sold and vegetables, such as beans, cabbages, turnips, radishes, carrots, onions and leeks. Leeks were very popular both for their own sake and because they were used for flavouring. Many herbs of different kinds were grown, such as sage, mint, fennel, parsley, marjoram and basil, and added to potage (a thick meaty soup).

Bread was a staple part of the diet for all but the wealthy and was still important for them too. It was thus important that it was widely available at a reasonable price so that even the poor could buy enough to live on. The Assize of Bread and Ale (for ale see below), a national law, laid down that a loaf was supposed to sell for 1d, the size varying according to the price of grain. This variation in size applied to bread of all types, that is a farthing loaf of the best bread would weigh half as much as the next quality, which in turn weighed half as much as the third quality. Thus a poor customer could get a loaf four times as large as a richer customer for the same price, albeit of poorer quality. A penny loaf was quite large though and most people, the poorer ones certainly, usually wanted smaller loaves, down to the farthing loaf. These small loaves were not popular with the bakers who sometimes refused to sell farthing loaves. Bread was sold in several different qualities from the very best white to the cheapest quality which was made from flour with nothing removed, thus containing all of the bran. The enforcement of the Assize lay with the town authorities of each place, who altered the weight of the loaf as the price of grain changed. It was necessary to keep a firm control over bakers because of their potential power: a strike by them such as did occur in some towns would deprive a town of its main staple food.

Food was also bought from strolling hucksters. In all towns 'hucksters', frequently women, were allowed to sell bread from house to house. These 'hucksters' (or 'byrlesters') seem to have made their profit from being allowed by law to receive thirteen batches for every twelve bought, a 'bakers dozen'. They were supposed to sell only while passing through the streets, i.e. were not supposed to stand still and sell although sometimes they could stand and sell their goods if they paid for the privilege. Some itinerant salesmen also sold shellfish and salt fish. Non food sellers, traveling salesmen known as chapmen, have been described earlier.

Food was not only bought raw but could easily be brought ready cooked too. Many shops sold ready prepared food, although not ale which they were forbidden to sell. Cookshops sold roast birds, including small birds such as thrushes and various finches, roast meat of various kinds, and geese, hens and capons baked in pastry. These were fairly expensive and not something that the ordinary household could afford every day, although perhaps they would do so on special occasions. It would take a craftsman more than two days to earn the cost of a capon in pastry, or two days without the pastry. It would only cost him a half a day's wages for 'paste, fire and trouble upon a capon' if he provided the capon. Roast rabbit and best roasted lamb were more reasonably priced but still not something that the less affluent family could buy often. Sauces and puddings were also sold. These cookshops seem originally at least to have supplied meals in the customer's house if required. Everything for a good meal could be bought in fact. These 'ready meals' were popular partly because many houses had no adequate kitchen or cooking facilities and partly because the best way to keep food, particularly in the summer, was to cook it. They were also very useful when unexpected guests had to be fed. Food retailers were usually not allowed to combine two trades, for example cooks and piebakers (a related trade) were usually forbidden to sell raw food (this was encroaching on the trade of others such as butchers) or to keep hostels for the entertainment of guests and travelers, this was the prerogative of the tavern keeper. From the food point of view the medieval poem London Lickpenny shows what was available to the traveller or citizen who could afford the middle ages equivalent of fast food and gives a vivid picture of a medieval street.

Then to Westminster gate I went
when the sun was at high prime
Cook to me they took good intent
called me near for to dine
and proffered me good bread ale and wine
a fair cloth they began to spread
ribs of beef both fat and fine
but for lack of money I might not speed
In to London I began to go
of all the land it beareth the prize
hot peascods one began to cry

> strawberry ripe and cherry in the ryse
> one bade me come near and buy some spice
> pepper and saffron they offered me
> cloves, grains and flour of rice
> for lack of money I might not speed

The narrator is later offered hot sheep's feet, ribs of beef, 'many a pie' and mackerel.

As well as food, something to drink was also important. Milk was an important part of the diet and was bought from farms within or just outside the walls or from shops where the owner kept a cow on a small piece of ground. The quality must have been very variable and it would have gone off very quickly in the summer. Another important part of the diet and also a part of communal and social life, was ale, that is unhopped beer – beer with hops was not common until the sixteenth century. Ale was the main drink since water was usually of doubtful purity and the brewing process made it safer. The law checked the quality of ale as well as bread and in this case the price of ale was tied to the price of the barley from which it was made. The amount of ale bought for a penny thus varied with the price of barley. Even so it was frequently the case that a penny would buy as much as a gallon of ale. Ale was sold in ale houses (which were basically shops which (usually) brewed their own ale) or sometimes merely private homes, and in taverns which also sold food and wine and let rooms to guests. The small scale operations were financially possible because ale was best drunk near where it was brewed since it went off quickly. Very many of the small scale ale sellers were female, since brewing was one of the few trades open to women. Poorer 'alewives' who could not afford the outlay necessary to brew for themselves would buy ale to resell.

Taverns were usually on a much larger scale than the ale houses, sometimes very large indeed and together with alehouses were marked with a 'bush' to show their trade. The bush was a pole, an 'alestake', projecting from the building, on the end of which was a bunch of leaves or sometimes an actual bush. Sometimes other signs were also used, names of inns such as The Sun, The Mermaid and The Boar are known. The 'bushes' were sometimes a great nuisance and towns made ordinances complaining that the alestakes sometimes projected so far over the highway as to impede the progress of riders and forbidding this. Their weight also caused the houses to deteriorate. In London it was ordered that no one should have an alestake projecting over the king's highway by more than seven feet 'on pain of paying a fine to the Mayor and Aldermen'. Seven feet was possibly the width of the footpath in the wider thoroughfares, although it seems rather a lot. The alestake also had another meaning, an announcement that a new brew had been made, and was a request for the aleconner to come and visit the premises. The aleconner was appointed by the town authorities to go and taste the ale to check the quality. There were very many taverns and even more ale houses although ale selling was frequently informal, from the doorway of the brewer for example. Whether formal or informal they were always a focus of informal social groups of all levels where townsfolk could take their ease. From the housewife with her group of 'gossips' to the priests whose superiors frequently had to tell not to hang around alehouses and taverns.

Water was the drink of those who could afford little else. Most towns were near a river and this would be used as a water supply by those lucky enough to be near it. As towns grew, this would be difficult and in any case the water would be increasingly polluted. Most towns had public wells where inhabitants could get water although a few houses had their own private well. The public wells were the responsibility of the town authorities who were supposed to keep them usable and in good condition. Keeping public water supplies pure and usable by ordinary citizens and stopping various tradesmen from misusing the pure water was a constant battle. Thus a continual effort had to be made by town authorities to prevent the brewers from monopolising the public supplies as a source of good clean water for making their ale as well as preventing the fishmongers from washing their fish or tanners their hides. Even at the best of times the water probably would not be what we would regard as pure.

Some large towns had public conduits of fresh water piped into the town to a convenient point or points. These were sometimes paid for out of bequests or in some cases the town arranged with a religious house to share with the town or allow it to take over the conduit the house had built for themselves. The water from these points was always reasonably fresh and clean and was more useful as a supply than a well since it could have outlets at a convenient height for jars and containers to be filled without great effort. They were also safer. Accidents in which children and even adults fell down wells and were drowned are sadly not uncommon in town records. The conduits were unfortunately open to abuse by both tradesmen and householders. It was not unknown for a householder to wash themselves or their clothes at the public supply. Others merely tapped the pipe at a higher point away from the official outlet and gave themselves a private water supply. This was severely punished if discovered.

In all towns water was also supplied (at a charge) by water carriers who may have taken it from the relatively pure conduits or from the local river (if close enough). These water carriers had rounds rather like a modern milkman and were jealous of rivals who tried to steal their customers. They delivered water in jars although they also used water carts. They charged their customers presumably by the size of the container delivered and sometimes suffered bad debts which they had to go to the courts to recover. Their major customers were probably tradesmen such as the brewers who used very large amounts of fresh water. These water carriers together with householders collecting their own water and carefully carrying a large full jar through the crowded streets would have been a very common sight. Going to the conduit head or the public well and meeting neighbours was an important part of social life for most housewives and perhaps the men too.

CHAPTER 8

Markets

Markets were a very important part of life in a medieval town both as part of the economy, employing many of the citizens, and providing an outlet for goods made or brought in. When they were in full swing they must have been indescribably noisy places with merchants shouting their wares, the noise of chickens and geese waiting to be sold and the noise of the iron clad wheels of the carts bringing in more goods. Markets also brought income for the town itself in the payment of tolls which traders had to pay for the right to have a stall in the market. The market itself was usually in a square or other open space in the town, or sometimes in a wide street, and consisted of open stalls. Very often the stalls were temporary ones and were taken down when trading finished for the day. Wherever markets were held they were strictly regulated in the days, times and places where they could be held. The controls began outside the town because suppliers were forbidden to sell goods to anyone outside the town, to forestallers as they were known, who could then sell privately at a higher price without the goods ever reaching the market. Traders bringing goods to the market were also forced to sell in the official market and not wander the streets of the town selling directly to their customers and saving themselves the market fee.

Trading began very early, certainly by 6a.m the market would be in full swing. Sometimes traders were allowed to sell such goods as geese, hens and chickens before this, but only for private consumption. After 6a.m traders could sell to professional cooks or resellers. Great efforts were made to ensure that town residents had an advantage and were sometimes allowed to supply and buy goods in the mornings, whereas foreigners, that is non townspeople, were only allowed to do so in the afternoon. Sometimes the hour at which foreigners could begin to trade was announced by a particular church bell. The opening and closing of the market was announced by the ringing of yet another bell.

An important part of the regulation of markets (as well as other trading) was that prices and quality were checked by the authorities. The price of bread and ale for example were regulated by the Assize of Bread and Ale as we saw above, and other goods were regulated too. It may have been more necessary in a market but checking quality was something that went on all the time everywhere, for all goods, not just foodstuffs. Every guild had to appoint two searchers. This was a very important office in the guild and gave the holders the right to enter private premises if necessary to examine goods. They could fine transgressors heavily if they were found to have made substandard goods or had adulterated the goods they were selling. Selling bad quality food and adulteration of bread for example was severely frowned upon. The searchers were in turn firmly regulated, officials of such influence could not be left to chance, their appointment was controlled and frequently the mayor could appoint them without the intervention of the relevant guild. The accuracy of the weights by which goods were sold could be checked too if necessary by means of official weights and measures.

The most amazing variety of goods were sold in most markets and usually the buyer could find everything that they might need, either foodstuffs such as grain, butter, meat, fish and poultry, fruit, herbs and vegetables or goods for their business such as leather, linen and woollen cloth or jewellery and fine goods for themselves, all of them in the one place in a medieval version of a supermarket. Sometimes in a big town a particular market was chiefly reserved for one category of goods such as meat or grain or one or more days in a general market might be allocated to one category.

Not all of the trading in markets was on a large scale. Many of the smaller traders were people who had other trades, including priests trading for their own profit who might be selling their own or the tithes of fellow clergymen. Much of the trading in food was related to the trader's primary occupation, for example bakers or brewers might become involved in selling grain. It is probably true to say that virtually every household carried on any other business which had the skill or means to do, as well as the one by which they nominally made their living. Piece work in the textile and tailoring industries was the most common option for extra-mural jobs but crafts such as candle making and string making were also commonly practiced in this way. This was despite the nominal monopoly which each craft had over its own business since in practice this was impossible to enforce.

Women sometimes traded on their own account as well as helping with their husband's stall. Women were indeed occasionally major merchants, sometimes as the widow of a trader, which they were specifically allowed to do, or in partnership with a son or other relation.

The holding of fairs was also a very important part of the life of a town. These fairs were held at regular intervals not always actually in the town but always near a centre of population. They were very much bigger than the ordinary markets and usually took place over several days or even over weeks. The range of goods sold was always very much wider than in markets and was the main opportunity for people to buy fine wines, spices and such things as lace and perfumes not easily available normally. The bigger fairs were attended by foreign merchants bringing goods not often seen by people. Fairs were also places to watch strolling players, fire eaters, sword swallowers, acrobats and performing animals. The entertainers, who were an important part of the reason to visit the fairs, were usually professionals who made a living travelling from fair to fair. The noise at fairs must have been even greater than at a normal market.

CHAPTER 9

Religious Life

Religion was omnipresent in medieval life and towns had many religious buildings. There were many parish churches for example, in older towns parishes were usually very small and some towns had more than forty parishes. In addition to the parish churches there were often large churches and associated buildings belonging to one of the four orders of friars or other religious orders within the walls or just outside. As already noticed the bells from these churches rang frequently. Perhaps sometimes it seemed as though it was all the time.

The whole day and year was punctuated by the life of the church. Time was marked out by the bells ringing for the services throughout the day and marking the canonical hours, starting with Prime at about five or six o'clock and ending with Vespers and Compline between four and seven o'clock, probably bedtime in the winter. Townsfolk were able to regulate their days by these events, only approximately, but good enough for most purposes. Clocks were known throughout most of the middle ages but were expensive and not common. Secular events were reckoned by the church liturgical calendar, rents and leases were reckoned from the quarter days, Lady day, Lammas, Michaelmas and Christmas day. Anniversaries, legal deeds and birthdays were reckoned from the saint's days on which they occurred. The year was numbered from the accession of the current king as well as from the incarnation of Christ.

Every day mass was celebrated in churches with pageantry and many townspeople went regularly but there were many religious processions and events outside the church which provided colour and amusement for everyone. There were for example the Rogationtide processions. Rogation Sunday was the fifth Sunday after Easter. It was a time when the crops in the fields were blessed and processions went around the parish with bells, banners and the parish cross to drive out evil spirits and to bring good weather and fertility to the fields and even town parishes held these ceremonies. The processions went around the parish boundary to mark them in the memory of all, particularly the young, who were often beaten or otherwise maltreated to fix parish markers in their memory. They then shared in the ale and food that was provided at various places. The whole event was one which helped create a sense of parish community and shared enjoyment. Similar jollifications took place at other times, for example on the eves of the feasts of St John the Baptist, and St Thomas the Apostle when bonfires were lit and food was given to the poor. The Saint John feast took place at midsummer and took over from the pagan ceremonies of this time. The bonfires were probably not popular in towns because of the fire hazard they presented.

The parish provided an important focus for members of the community. It was the main centre for their devotional life and also their social life – they expressed their identity and cooperated with each other there. Both parishioners and priests were fiercely loyal to their parish and often left money in their wills for the beautification of their church, for example by giving enough money to erect a new stained glass window. Sometimes the parish raised enough to rebuild the church.

An important part of religious activity was provided by the religious guilds or fraternities. These were not necessarily connected to craft guilds although all of these had a religious dimension too. The religious guild was partly a social club for people within a particular community and partly a friendly society but always within the ambit of the church, frequently a single parish. Members paid a fee to join and some of the money was used to arrange for the burial of a dead member with members attending the funeral, going in procession to the grave and distributing alms. All of these spiritual services were important for members who might well not be able to pay for them properly for themselves. Members of the guild went together to church on Sundays and at other times too. Ceremonial occasions such as the feast of the guild's patron saint were marked by processions, and the distribution of alms. Almsgiving was an important religious duty. Money for these activities came from entry fees to the guild and was also raised by holding feasts regularly. Richer members sometimes gave property to the guild or left it money. From these gifts successful guilds ran schools, hospitals and almshouses and members could benefit from all of these if they needed them. The guilds provided a social circle for members, they always provided feasts, as well as sometimes loans in time of need or help in legal troubles. They also frequently gave charitable help to the wider community. As well as being a religious duty charity to others was a practical duty. Everyone knew how easy it was to become destitute through ill luck or illness and so would know how important it was to contribute towards charitable giving. Most religious guilds allowed anyone to become a member, women included. Some guilds were very small and their activities might be limited to supporting parish services and even just maintaining an altar light in their parish church. It would nonetheless still be a vehicle to express membership of the community, giving support in this world and in the next.

An important part of the religious life of a guild was the provision of masses for dead members. Mediaeval religion laid stress on the efficacy of the mass as one of the good works which were necessary for an individual's salvation. If a citizen was rich enough they would pay a priest to say mass or a number of masses on their behalf when they were dead. Men and women often left money in their wills to pay for these masses to be said on their behalf to shorten their time in purgatory. Very rich guilds might set up their own chapel in their parish church for this but all of them purchased at least a share in a priest to say masses for their dead members. Thus if a person could not afford to pay for their own masses they joined such a religious guild which purchased a share in a priest who would say masses for the dead and for the members of the fraternity every Sunday. In towns there were many unbeneficed priests who were not officially attached to a parish but nevertheless were unofficially part of it. They had no regular income and welcomed patrons for whom they could say mass and so provide themselves with an income. Since they were all literate they could also write wills ad other documents for anyone and increase their income in that way too.

In some towns these religious guilds also took part in an annual cycle of religious plays, the mystery plays. Each guild performed the same play each year and there was much rivalry between guilds as to who could put on the best production. The craft guilds also took part in these cycles. The plays were important because they provided religious instruction for the masses, the big Corpus Christi cycle in York for example told the story of the bible from the creation to the last judgement and many guilds, fraternal and craft took part as did the masons, not normally part of a guild network. These plays also provided popular entertainment and were always enthusiastically received. They incorporated within them popular stories to make the text more memorable, the story of Noah for example included Noah's shrewish wife.

Schools were another service provided by the church or by individual priests. Keeping a school was another way for an unbeneficed priest to earn a living. These schools were open to all who could pay and they took girls too sometimes. The education given was not exclusively religious, reading at least was taught and sometimes singing. Most education was purely elementary but some towns had grammar schools, initially run by the larger religious institutions such as monasteries or cathedrals but later by lay people.

Afterword

It is apparent that life in a medieval town was very different to that in a modern European town. There are a few similarities, just enough to show the essential continuity. Life in a town in the medieval period was more claustrophobic than now and the town was much smaller. Inside the walls the towns would to us resemble large villages in size and look rather like the centres of some old towns. In other ways medieval towns were like villages too, for example people were much more likely to meet friends or relations when out in the streets than anyone living in a modern town. The streets were very noisy with commercial activity, with shoppers, shopkeepers and itinerant street sellers calling out their wares. Modern streets are equally noisy, sometimes very noisy, but the noise is mechanical and totally unlike the human noise of the past. Some reminder of the noise of the past remained in recent memory with street sellers calling out their presence, particularly the rag and bone man and newspaper sellers, but these are mostly gone now. Open markets still exist in a few places but they are generally fairly sedate compared with their medieval counterparts. One of the main differences, one which fortunately cannot generally be paralleled nowadays, is the lack of cleanliness with a smell perhaps rather like a badly kept farmyard. Perhaps in the end the differences between then and now do greatly outweigh the similarities.

Select Bibliography

Frugoni, Chiara, *A Day in a Medieval City*, London, University of Chicago Press, 2006

Dyer, Christopher, *Standards of Living in the later Middle Ages,: Social change in England c. 1200-1520*, CUP, 1989

Gies, Joseph and Frances, *Life in a Medieval City*, New York, Harper & Row, 1969

Hammond, Peter, *Food and Feast in Medieval England*, second edition, Stroud, Sutton, 2005

Palliser, David, *Tudor York*, OUP, 1979

Salusbury, G. T., *Street Life in Medieval England*, second edition, Oxford, Pen-In Hand, 1948

Schofield, John, *The Building of London from the conquest to the Great Fire*, London, Colonnade Books, 1984

Swanson Heather, *Medieval British Towns*, Basingstoke, Macmillan, 1999

Thompson, Michael, *The Medieval Hall: The basis of secular domestic life, 600-1600 AD,* Aldershot, Scolar Press, 1995